Golda MEIR

ANNA CLAYBOURNE

Heinemann Library
Chicago, Illinois

Customer Service 888-454-2279

Visit our website at www.heinemannlibrary.com

Originated by Dot Gradations, Ltd.
Printed by South China Printing Company, Ltd.

07 06 05 04 03
10 9 8 7 6 5 4 3 2 1

Library of Congress Cataloging-in-Publication Data

Claybourne, Anna.
  Golda Meir / Anna Claybourne.
     v. cm. -- (Leading lives)
Includes bibliographical references and index.
Contents: Woman on a mission -- Poverty in Russia -- Being Jewish -- A
new world -- To Palestine! -- A new job -- Problems for Palestine -- War
and horror -- Israel is born! -- In government -- Israel's problems --
Prime minister Meir-- Golda Meir's legacy -- Timeline -- Key people of
Golda Meir's time.
  ISBN 1-40340-835-1 (Library Binding-hardcover)
  1. Meir, Golda, 1898-1978. 2. Prime
ministers--Israel--Biography--Juvenile literature. 3.
Israel--Biography--Juvenile literature. [1. Meir, Golda, 1898-1978. 2.
Prime ministers. 3. Women--Biography. 4. Israel--History.] I. Title.
II. Series.
  DS126.6.M42 C55 2003
  956.9405'3'092--dc21

2002012592

Acknowledgements
The author and publishers are grateful to the following for permission to reproduce copyright
material: pp. 4, 36, 37 Bettmann/Corbis; pp. 5, 7, 16, 17, 18 Golda Meir Library; pp. 6, 13, 40, 46
Topham Picturepoint; pp. 9, 43 Hulton Getty; p. 10 Richard T. Nowitz/Corbis; p. 15 Milwaukee
County Historical Society; pp. 20, 39, 49, 51, 53 Popperfoto; pp. 23, 26, 33 Hulton Archive; p. 29
Anthony Potter Collection/Hulton Archive; p. 31 Hulton Deutsch Collection/Corbis; pp. 34, 54
Corbis; pp. 44, 48, 52 David Rubinger/Corbis.

Cover photograph of Golda Meir reproduced with permission of Popperfoto.

Every effort has been made to contact copyright holders of any material reproduced in this book.
Any omissions will be rectified in subsequent printings if notice is given to the publisher.

Some words are shown in bold, **like this.** You can find out what they
mean by looking in the glossary.

Contents

Woman on a Mission

The year was 1969, and the United States was preparing for a grand state visit. Organizers planned banquet menus, bands rehearsed, and the White House rolled out the red carpet. When the guest of honor arrived, a crowd of more than 30,000 people had gathered to greet her. Wherever she went, people hailed her as a hero. Her name was Golda Meir.

◀ *Golda Meir appears with President Richard Nixon outside the White House during her state visit to the United States in 1969. Although a series of scandals later forced Nixon out of office, Meir always supported him in return for his help when she became Israel's prime minister.*

In her youth, Meir had lived in Milwaukee, Wisconsin. Now, she was the leader of the young state of Israel located in the Middle East. She had come back to the United States, which supported Israel, to ask for help. Her country was engaged in constant **skirmishes** with its neighbors and needed money and arms to defend its borders.

Leading the way

Golda Meir was not everyone's idea of a world leader. A small lady at the age of 70, she was already a grandmother when she took over the leadership of Israel in March 1969. At first, she had taken the job temporarily after the death of Prime Minister Levi Eshkol. She had planned to stand in until the

▶ *Students welcome Prime Minister Meir to her old hometown of Milwaukee in 1969.*

government could hold elections later that year. Her colleagues asked her to stay on, and she ended up leading Israel for more than five years.

At the time, Meir was only the third woman in the world to be elected prime minister in any country (after Sirimavo Bandaranaike of Sri Lanka in 1960 and Indira Gandhi of India in 1966). Not only did she lead Israel, but she was also one of the people who had helped to found the new country just twenty years earlier.

Strong beliefs

All her life, Meir wanted one thing more than any other—to create a peaceful **homeland** for the Jewish people. She struggled endlessly to make that dream a reality. Her heartfelt belief in the rights of the Jewish people and her incredible energy drove her. Her stubborn devotion to her task made her many enemies. Yet, her iron will and powerful **charisma** made her one of the best leaders in history.

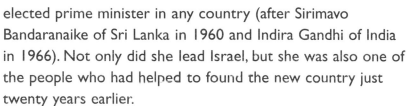

Woman at the top

Golda Meir never felt that being a woman should stop her from succeeding. During her political career, interviewers often asked her how it felt to be a woman minister. She would reply innocently: "I do not know—I have never been a man minister."

Poverty in Russia

Golda Meir spent the first eight years of her life in Russia. She was born Golda Mabovitch on May 3, 1898, in Kiev (now part of the Ukraine). At the age of three, her family moved to Pinsk (now in Belarus).

Golda's father Moshe Mabovitch worked as a carpenter. Her mother Blume was employed to care for other people's children. But they were still very poor. Later in life, Meir remembered that during her childhood "there was never enough of anything . . . I was always a little too cold outside and a little too empty inside." She hated having to share her food with her baby sister Zipke. Their big sister Shenya often fainted from hunger. The family lived in a single room. These terrible living conditions meant that five of the Mabovitches' children—four boys and a girl—died before they reached their first birthdays. Only Shenya, Golda, and Zipke survived.

◀ This picture, taken in Putilov, Russia, shows the dirty and cramped conditions in which many poorer members of society lived at the end of the 1800s.

Discrimination

One reason life was so hard was that Golda and her family were Jewish. Jews were a religious minority in Russia with their own traditions. Because they were different, many people hated and feared them. Russia forced Jews to live in their own areas, away from other Russians, who were mainly Christians. Although Golda's father was a good carpenter, he found it difficult to find work, because people did not want to employ Jews and **discriminated** against them.

The pogroms

Worst of all, gangs of people massacred large numbers of Jewish people in violent attacks called **pogroms.** Rioters would charge through Jewish areas, attacking, wounding, and even killing Jewish people and destroying their homes. The **czar** turned a blind eye to the pogroms, and his **cossacks** sometimes even joined the attackers.

The pogroms terrified Golda, but they also deeply puzzled her. Why would anyone want to hurt her just because of her religion? When she saw her father boarding up their front door because of the pogroms, this angered her. She thought it was no good simply to hide away. Even as a small child, Golda believed a better way existed for Jewish people to save themselves from this nightmare.

▲ Golda Mabovitch, as a six-year-old girl, poses for this picture.

A cossack attack

When Golda was five years old and living in Pinsk, she went to play with friends near a swamp called the *blotte*. A band of cossacks came galloping toward them on their horses. Instead of stopping, they rode straight over the crouching children, not caring if they trampled them to death. Golda survived, but she never went near the *blotte* again.

The horror of a pogrom

"It is impossible to account the amounts of goods destroyed in a few hours. The hurrahs of the rioting. The pitiful cries of the victims filled the air. Wherever a Jew was met he was savagely beaten into insensibility [unconsciousness]. One Jew was dragged from a streetcar and beaten until the mob thought he was dead. The air was filled with feathers and torn bedding. Every Jewish household was broken into and the unfortunate Jews in their terror endeavored [tried] to hide in cellars and under roofs."

(An eyewitness account of a pogrom in Kishinev, Russia, in April 1903, printed in the *New York Times*)

An American dream

In 1903, discouraged by his failure to make a good living in Russia, Moshe Mabovitch decided to go to the United States. He was sure it would be easier to find work there, and he could save money and send it home to his family. Meanwhile, Blume and the three girls stayed with Blume's parents in Pinsk.

At that time, people from all over the world, including more than a million Jews, were going to the United States to make their fortunes. They believed they could find better lives for themselves and for their families. Although many people did build better lives, succeeding was not always as easy as they expected. Golda's father struggled for three years before finding a job that could support his family. Left behind in Pinsk, they only survived with help from Golda's grandfather. They moved into an apartment above a bakery, and Golda's mother got a job there. Life was still hard.

Shenya's secrets

As she grew older, Golda realized that Shenya was keeping secrets from the rest of her family. Shenya was nine years older than Golda. She would disappear to mysterious meetings and come home late. She had huge arguments with their mother, who seemed terrified for her safety.

Hiding on top of the stove or pretending to be asleep, Golda would listen in when her sister's friends came to the house. She discovered that Shenya belonged to a political movement that wanted to make things better for the Jews. Sometimes they talked about overthrowing the **czar,** but mostly they dreamed of starting a new, independent country in which Jews could live. This idea was growing among Jewish people around the world. People called the idea **Zionism,** after *Zion,* an old Hebrew word for the Jewish people and their **homeland.**

In Russia, the government made belonging to member of a **Zionist** group against the law. If authorities had caught Shenya, they would have arrested and punished her. Blume was afraid for her daughter, but she could not force her to give up her political activities. So, in 1905, she wrote to her husband saying that they had to leave Russia. They were going to join him in the United States.

◀ *Immigrants await medical examination at Ellis Island, New York, in 1904. Most people who moved to the United States from Europe had to be processed here before being allowed to enter the country.*

Being Jewish

From an early age, Golda Meir realized that she was in a **minority.** Although her family was not especially religious, Jewish traditions played a big part in their lives. Instead of the Christian festivals most Russians and Europeans celebrated, Golda and her family celebrated Jewish holidays such as Passover, Hanukkah, and Yom Kippur. Golda's family also spoke in a traditional Jewish language called **Yiddish** and ate only kosher food. The religious laws of keeping kosher forbid some foods, such as shellfish and pork.

◀ *A Jewish family in Israel celebrates Passover with a special meal called the Seder. Passover is one of the most important Jewish holidays.*

In Russia, the government only allowed Jewish people to live in a certain area of the country (known as the Pale of Settlement). They also lived in specific Jewish areas within each town, called **ghettos.** The government crowded jews into ghettos and gave them poor housing. However, the ghettos gave Jewish people a strong sense of community. Generations of Jews had handed down traditional recipes, folk music, and religious rituals over hundreds of years. Jewish people socialized only among their own kind and only married other Jews. This is the kind of close-knit atmosphere in which Golda Meir spent her childhood.

"Next year in Jerusalem"

Every year, like most Jews, Golda and her family celebrated the Jewish festival of Passover. This holiday remembers the **exodus** of Jews from slavery in Egypt. Jews read the story of their ancestors' desire for freedom during the festivities, and they chant the words *"L'shanah ha-baah bi Yerushalayim"*—"Next year in Jerusalem." This is because, more than 2,000 years ago, the Jewish people had their own kingdom centered around the holy city of Jerusalem. According to the Bible, God promised this land to the Jews, or **Hebrews,** as they were then known.

▲ *This map shows the original Jewish homeland about 800 B.C.E. It was split into two areas, one called Israel and the other called Judah.*

However, because of various wars and conquests, most Jews were eventually forced to leave. Golda's ancestors ended up in Russia, but Jews settled in many other countries, especially in Eastern Europe. Historians call this scattering of Jewish people around the world the Jewish **diaspora.** Although they made new lives elsewhere, most Jews preserved their traditional beliefs and continued to view Jerusalem as their spiritual home—a home to which, one day, they would return.

Time to go home?

Golda Meir was born at the end of the 1800s. In earlier centuries, most Jews had held a traditional belief that their **messiah,** or divine leader, would appear and lead them back to the **promised land.** But by Golda's time, ideas had begun to change. People started saying that, instead of waiting for a messiah, Jews should make the return to the promised land themselves. At that time, the old land of the **Hebrews** was called Palestine. It was part of the **Ottoman Empire.** Perhaps Jews could turn Palestine back into a **homeland** for the Jewish people?

FOR DETAILS ON KEY PEOPLE OF MEIR'S TIME, SEE PAGE 58.

A movement begins

Many people felt an urgent need for a Jewish homeland because anti-Semitism—hatred of Jews—was causing so much suffering. For centuries other groups, especially Christians, had disliked the Jews and accused them of being mean, dishonest, and simply different. Now, the prejudice and **persecution** seemed to be growing even worse. Around Europe, Jews such as Golda's sister, Shenya, discussed what should be done, and the plan for a homeland began to take shape.

A Hungarian Jew named Theodor Herzl wrote a booklet called *The Jewish State.* In 1897, at a Jewish conference in Basel, Switzerland, he founded a society called the World **Zionist** Organization, which planned to find a Jewish homeland. By 1900, **Zionism** was a major force in Eastern Europe, and the first European Jews had already settled in Palestine.

Theodor Herzl

Theodor Herzl was born in Hungary in 1860. He later moved to
Vienna, the capital of Austria. From there, he worked as a
newspaper reporter in Paris, France. The anti-Semitism Herzl saw
there outraged him. He wrote books and organized meetings to
discuss the creation of a Jewish state. He was a hero to young
Zionists in the early 1900s, when Golda Meir and her sisters were
growing up. After Herzl died in 1904, many Jews sat *shiva*, a
traditional period of mourning for seven days. Golda's sister Shenya
wore black mourning clothes for two years.

▲ *Theodor Herzl (center) and some of his followers traveled to Palestine
in 1898.*

A New World

Golda would one day go to Palestine herself. Before that, however, she had to make another huge move. She and her family were preparing to leave their old life behind and join Moshe in Milwaukee.

Today, a person can fly from Europe to the United States in several hours. But in 1906, for a poor family from Russia, the journey took weeks. First, Golda's mother had to bribe the police to let them leave Russia. When they reached Galicia (now part of Poland), they had to hide in a ice cold shack for two days, waiting for a train to take them to the coast. After waiting another two days in Belgium, they finally boarded a ship for the fourteen-day journey across the Atlantic Ocean. They traveled in **steerage,** the lowest and cheapest class, with eight people crammed into each tiny cabin.

Culture shock

Throughout the journey, Golda wondered what Milwaukee would be like. But the reality was beyond anything she could have imagined. She was overwhelmed and amazed by the United States—the huge buildings, the amazing variety of shops to visit and things to buy, and the bright colors of street advertisements and people's clothes. Golda had never seen so many vehicles on the streets—she had never even been in a car before. She loved it.

However, it was difficult for the family to live together again after so long. Moshe had changed. He had new American friends and clothes and had learned English. He wanted his family to change, too. Golda and Zipke were young enough to accept this, but Shenya hated it. The move had forced her to leave her boyfriend Shamai behind in Pinsk, and she missed her home terribly.

Settling in

Although they were still poor, life was easier in the United States. Moshe had found work with a railway company, and Blume decided to set up her own general store. Golda started school, which she loved, and made a new best friend named Regina Hamburger. Many Jewish people lived in Milwaukee, and this friendly community embraced the Mabovitch family.

Memories of Milwaukee

In her autobiography, *My Life*, Meir wrote about her amazement and excitement when she arrived in the United States. "I was delighted by my pretty new clothes, by the soda pop and ice cream," she recalled. "Everything looked so colorful and fresh, as though it had just been created."

▲ To eight-year-old Golda Mabovitch, who had spent her life in poverty and had never seen a tall building or ridden in a car, Milwaukee—pictured above in the 1900s—seemed like a different universe.

Politics and Palestine

By the early 1900s, many Eastern European Jews, including those now in Milwaukee, were talking about **Zionism.** The Mabovitches' small apartment was always full of friends and neighbors, discussing and debating the Palestine issue over endless glasses of tea. Influenced by these discussions, Golda found herself thinking about Zionism more and more. She knew that more and more Jews were moving to Palestine to start a Jewish **homeland** there. And she knew that someday she would like to join them.

Running away

Shenya became sick with **tuberculosis,** and doctors sent her to Denver, Colorado, to recover. She set up home there with Shamai, who had come to the United States to be with her. At home in Milwaukee, the teenage Golda became increasingly annoyed with her parents. They wanted her to work in their shop and marry a man who was twice her age. But Golda wanted to stay in school. How could she help to build a Jewish state if she did not have a good education?

▼ *Golda Mabovitch poses with her classmates in 1912 at the age of fourteen. She is on the far right of the photo, wearing a white blouse.*

▲ Golda (far right) taught at a Yiddish school in the Jewish Center in Milwaukee in 1916 when she was eighteen years old.

She wrote countless letters to Shenya complaining about her situation. Finally, when Golda was fifteen years old, Shenya said she could come and live with her. Shenya and Shamai sent the money for a train ticket and, with Regina Hamburger's help, Golda ran away from home. She did not stay in Denver for long, but the experience gave her her first taste of freedom. Listening to Shenya's friends talking about politics every night made her even more sure of her **Zionist** beliefs. She also fell in love.

Meeting Morris

Morris Meyerson was one of the many friends who visited Shenya and Shamai's home. He was quiet, shy, and studious. He introduced Golda to art, literature, and classical music and gave her books to read. When, just a year later, Golda decided to go home to Milwaukee, Morris told her he wanted to marry her.

Back home

When Golda returned to Milwaukee in 1915, her parents were so happy to have her back that they allowed her to stay in school. There, she became even more committed to her political beliefs. In addition to campaigning for the **Zionist** cause, Golda was a **socialist.** She believed in trying to make things better for the poor. She often organized events to raise money for charity. As a woman, she was not allowed to speak in the synagogue (the Jewish house of worship), so she stood on a box outside and made impassioned speeches about **socialism** and **Zionism.** Although her actions annoyed Moshe, as a Zionist himself he could not help but admire her devotion.

However, Golda's boyfriend, Morris, did not share her views. He liked his life in the United States and was not interested in

Zionism. In a move typical of the stubbornness she would show throughout her life, Golda told him she would not compromise. She was going to Palestine with or without him. Unable to bear the thought of losing her, Morris said he would follow her anywhere. So, in 1917, when Golda was just nineteen years old, Golda and Morris married.

◄ *Golda Mabovitch is shown here in 1917, the year she married Morris Meyerson.*

▮ To Palestine!

In 1917, World War I, which had started in 1914, was near its end. During the war, Britain had conquered Palestine. On November 2, 1917, the British foreign secretary Arthur Balfour made a historic statement. He said that Britain favored a Jewish **homeland** in Palestine. This statement became known as the Balfour Declaration, and Zionists around the world welcomed it. Now that they could count on Britain's help, many Jews started preparing to set off for the **promised land.** Golda and Morris were among them.

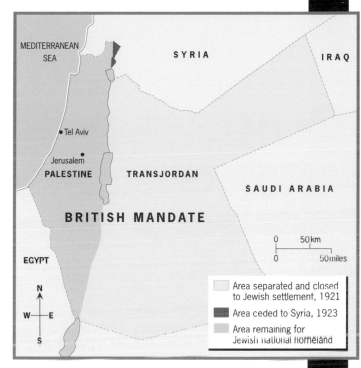

▲ This map shows the areas that the British mandate set aside for Jewish settlement after World War I.

Why did Britain set up a Jewish homeland in Palestine?

In the 1800s and early 1900s, Britain controlled many parts of the world, such as India, South Africa, and Palestine. In those days, British politicians believed they had a right to do whatever they wanted with the lands they ruled. As a result, they saw no problem with giving Palestinian land to the Jews. They also knew that people in many countries attacked and persecuted Jews, and they thought that a Jewish homeland would offer them protection.

Who are the Arabs?

The **Arabs** are a group of people who are mostly **Muslims.** They live in and around the Arabian **Peninsula** and across North Africa in countries such as Egypt, Syria, Iraq, Saudi Arabia, and Israel. During the early 1900s, most people living in Palestine were Arabs, and many of them resented the Jews claiming Palestine as the Jewish **homeland.** Much tension still exists between the Arabs and Jews today.

Leaving the United States

They were not traveling alone. Regina Hamburger and another friend, Yossel Kopelov, joined them. Shenya said she would come with her two children, leaving Shamai to follow

▼ *This photo shows a street in Tel Aviv in 1921, at the time when Golda, Morris, and Shenya arrived in Palestine.*

later. Their families were worried about their safety. The Arab people who lived in Palestine did not welcome the Jewish settlers. Sometimes Arabs killed Jews in anti-Jewish riots and Arab attacks. But they had made their decision, and on May 23, 1921, the party set off from New York on board the U.S.S. *Pocahontas*.

FOR A MAP OF THE PLACES MENTIONED, SEE PAGE 19.

To Tel Aviv

Golda and Morris's journey to Palestine was nightmarish. The crew of their ship had a **mutiny,** the boat almost sank, and the captain took his own life. Nevertheless, the group finally arrived in Italy and from there took another ship to Egypt and a train to Tel Aviv. Jewish settlers had founded this city in 1909. They were constantly adding new buildings, but the American newcomers found the life there shockingly basic. No grass grew—the houses stood on scorching desert sand— and many people lived in huts or tents. Flies crawling all over the food in the market even horrified usually tough Shenya.

Although they soon found an apartment, and Golda took a job teaching English, they all felt disappointed. Golda did not want a teaching job—she wanted to work on the land and help the settlers to feed themselves. So, she and Morris applied to join a **kibbutz,** or **communal** farm.

Kibbutz life

Kibbutz Merhavia in northern Palestine eventually accepted Golda and Morris. There, the other people on the kibbutz expected them to live communally, to do hard farm work, and to share basic food and sparse living space with 40 other members. They also had to learn **Hebrew,** the ancient Jewish language, which people were reviving.

Kibbutzim

The first Jewish settlers in Palestine set up communal farms called *kibbutzim* (the plural of *kibbutz*) to turn the poor and dry land into productive soil. The people living on a kibbutz based life there on the **socialist** ideals of sharing and equality. Inside a kibbutz, everyone had to share the work, space, food, and child care. When the **United Nations** (UN) officially created the Jewish state of Israel in 1948, the kibbutzim stayed, and many still exist today.

At first, the other **kibbutz** members thought the Americans would be too soft and spoiled for the kibbutz. But Golda threw herself into her work and grew to love her new way of life. She raised chickens, cleared stones from the soil, planted trees, and cooked in the kitchens. She also turned out to be a natural leader, and the kibbutz was always electing her to various committees. The kibbutz even sent her to represent Merhavia at conferences where the future of the **Yishuv** (the Jewish settlement in Palestine) was discussed. There, she met the leaders of the **Zionist** movement, and her interest in politics grew and grew.

Morris's misery

With every day that passed, Golda felt happier and more convinced that she was doing the right thing with her life. But for her husband, the opposite was true. Kibbutz life did not suit Morris at all. He liked privacy, books, art, and classical music, not shared living spaces and manual labor. He thought the Merhavia members were too serious and did not appreciate his intelligence and sense of humor. He was not good at farm work, and the hot weather made him sick. He finally said that if he and Golda wanted children, he did not

▲ *Jewish women work on a kibbutz in Palestine in the 1920s, as Golda and Morris did after moving there.*

want them to be brought up on a kibbutz. So, in 1924 Golda gave in and did what her husband wanted. She agreed to return to the city.

To Jerusalem

At first, Morris and Golda went back to Tel Aviv to stay with Shenya, but they could not find good jobs. Then David Remez, one of the Yishuv leaders Golda had befriended, offered them jobs in Jerusalem. They were to work for the **Histadrut,** the Jewish labor union, which organized Jewish **immigration** to Palestine, trained the new arrivals, and found them jobs.

The day before they left for Jerusalem, Golda discovered that she was pregnant. It seemed like a good sign, and the couple set off for their new lives with hope in their hearts.

The Jerusalem housewife

Golda's baby son Menachem was born on November 23, 1924. After his birth, Golda tried to settle into life as a stay-at-home mother. She caught up with her old friend Regina, who had moved to Jerusalem in 1921, and spent her days shopping and cooking. Although they only had a tiny apartment, with no electricity or running water and a tin shack in the yard for a kitchen, the situation still made Morris happy. In May 1926, their daughter Sarah was born, and in the same year, Golda's parents moved to Palestine, too. Almost her whole family now lived in Palestine (only Zipke, who had changed her name to Clara, remained in the United States).

Try as she might, Golda could not settle into a life tied to the home. Although she adored her children, she hated being a homemaker. She was desperate to work—not just anywhere—but at the heart of the movement to build a Jewish nation.

A woman's choice

When Menachem was born, Golda realized that she had a conflict in her life. "I had to decide which came first," she later wrote, "my duty to my husband, my home, and my child, or the kind of life I myself really wanted." To begin with, she chose duty, but it was not to last.

6 A New Job

Golda Meyerson spent four years in Jerusalem trying to make her marriage work, but for her they were unhappy years. She loved Morris, but her personality was so different from his that trying to live the life he wanted made her miserable.

Golda sometimes visited Shenya and her family in Tel Aviv. She also went to see her parents, who lived near Tel Aviv in a town called Herzlia. In 1928, on one of these trips, Golda's old friend David Remez saw her talking to a friend outside the **Histadrut** offices. He went up to her and asked if she would like to return to work—as the secretary of the Histadrut's Women's Labor Council.

The leaders of the Histadrut knew what Golda had to offer. Her passionate commitment to the cause, her natural political ability, and her incredible capacity for hard work made her invaluable. But if she took the job it would mean separating from Morris and going to live in Tel Aviv. She said yes.

Separation

Golda knew that her marriage was not working. Reluctantly, she told Morris that they were too different from each other and wanted different things. Although they were to remain friends, Golda knew she had to put her career first. She took the children, left Morris, and moved to Tel Aviv.

Her new job involved training female settlers for **kibbutz** work and organizing jobs for them. She also traveled abroad to tell other Jewish women's organizations about the **Yishuv.** Golda loved the job and threw herself into her new responsibilities, but she felt guilty about being a working mother. At the time, few mothers worked outside the home, and Golda's own mother and Shenya often told her that she was neglecting Menachem and Sarah. So, she spent every spare second with them, getting up early and staying up late to cook for them, play with them, and take them to clubs, concerts, or doctors' appointments. She worried endlessly about whether they were being harmed by her career.

▼ Jewish people arrive in Haifa, Palestine, about 1929. As a member of the Histadrut, Golda Meyerson was involved with recruiting such immigrants and finding them jobs when they arrived.

New friends

At the **Histadrut** offices in Tel Aviv, Golda formed close relationships with many of the most powerful people in Jewish Palestine. Men who, like her, would one day be Israel's leaders made up her circle. David Ben-Gurion, David Remez, Berl Katznelson, Zalman Shazar, and Levi Eshkol were not only great friends, but they were also valuable contacts. Knowing them put Golda at the heart of power in the growing Jewish nation.

On her foreign travels, too, Golda mixed with politicians and important people from around the world. During trips to the United States and Great Britain, she sensed much support for the Jewish settlers. She hoped that she could help to achieve what she had always dreamed: to turn the **Yishuv**—the Jewish settlement—into a real country.

Key dates: marriage, motherhood, and career

1917	• December	Marriage to Morris Meyerson
1921	• July	The Meyersons arrive in Palestine
1921	• October	They start living at Kibbutz Merhavia
1924	• February	They move to Tel Aviv, then to Jerusalem to start a family
1924	• November	Birth of their son Menachem
1926	• May	Birth of their daughter Sarah
1928		Morris and Golda separate, and Golda moves to Tel Aviv to start her new job with the Histadrut

To the United States

In 1932, Sarah fell sick with a kidney disease. Morris and Golda did not think that the hospitals in Palestine would be able to help her. So, Golda arranged to visit the United States on behalf of the **Histadrut,** to raise money and support for the **Yishuv.** She took the children with her, and Sarah recovered at a hospital in New York.

They were to stay in the United States for two years. Golda's work there was a huge success. She was brilliant at campaigning, public speaking, and raising money for the Jewish cause. She also found fame as an international representative of Jewish Palestine.

On her return to Palestine in 1934, the Histadrut elected her to the **Va'ad Hapoel,** the Histadrut's **executive committee.** In effect, this made her one of the leaders of the Yishuv. Jewish Palestine had no other government except its faraway British rulers, and the Va'ad Hapoel had gradually grown into a kind of ruling body. For the next fifteen years, Golda would use this position to work toward making the Yishuv—or Israel, as it would come to be known—into an independent state.

People and politics

The Yishuv was a Jewish name for the large group of Jews who had settled in Palestine. Although they were not an official state yet, they tried to live together as a nation. The Histadrut started off as the labor union of the Yishuv, but it gradually turned into a kind of ruling political party. Va'ad Hapoel was the committee of politicians that controlled the Histadrut and so controlled the Yishuv.

7 Problems for Palestine

In the mid-1930s, the British still controlled Palestine. In 1917, the British government had said it was in favor of a Jewish **homeland** there—but would it keep its word? World events were about to put Britain's role in Palestine to a terrible test.

FOR DETAILS ON KEY PEOPLE OF MEIR'S TIME, SEE PAGE 58.

In Germany, Adolf Hitler, leader of the **Nazi Party,** had taken power. He blamed the Jews for Germany's problems and for its defeat in World War I. Once in power, Hitler showed the full extent of his hatred of the Jews. He began to turn against Jews and other **minorities,** creating laws and promoting ideas that **discriminated** against them. Jewish people started to flee Germany—and where better to go than their **promised land?** As the 1930s progressed, increasing numbers of Jews began to arrive in Palestine. The Histadrut welcomed them, but the British were not happy. They tried to discourage Jewish **immigration,** because large-scale fighting between **Arabs** and Jews in Palestine worried the British.

▶ A woman reads an anti-Jewish poster displayed in a shop window in Germany in 1933.

The rise of Hitler
At first, Hitler's Nazi Party promised to improve life for all Germans. It certainly improved the German economy, which had suffered following World War I. But the Nazi Party also supported the idea that some humans were better than others. Nazis treated Jews, black people, **gypsies,** and the disabled as less than human. Even so, the party was popular with many German people and rapidly gained power during the 1930s.

A plan for two countries

Britain's main concern was that **Arabs** who lived in and around Palestine would object to more Jewish settlers. Riots had already taken place, and Arab attacks were still killing Jewish settlers. In response, an underground Jewish fighting force, the **Haganah,** had formed. Palestinian Jews disagreed with one other about what to do. Golda Meyerson and many others on **Va'ad Hapoel** favored self-restraint (*havlaga*). In other words, they opposed making the violence worse. Those on the political **right wing** believed in answering the Arab attacks with violence.

In 1937, Britain came up with a plan for creating two separate states in Palestine—one for Arabs and one for Jews. But no one could agree about the plan, and nothing came of it. The future of Palestine was still unclear.

The white paper and war

In the late 1930s, Hitler's armies started to invade large areas of Europe. In the countries occupied by Germany—including Austria and Czechoslovakia—the Nazis drove Jews from their homes and took their businesses and jobs away. More and more refugees lined up to enter Palestine. But the British, afraid of upsetting the Arabs, decided to stop Jewish **immigration.** In May 1939, they released a **white paper** (a government document) proposing to limit the number of new arrivals to 15,000 Jews per year. After five years, the document said, Jewish immigration should stop altogether.

The white paper infuriated Golda and the other **Yishuv** leaders. Now the Jews had to deal with three forces—Hitler's Nazi regime, the Arab groups who were attacking

▲ *When the British 1939 white paper restricted Jewish immigration to Palestine, Jews protested against it in the streets of Jerusalem.*

settlers, and the British government. All these forces threatened their dream of a **homeland** open to all Jews.

In September 1939, Britain and France finally declared war on Germany, and World War II began. The **Histadrut** was ready for battle, too. As soon as it could, it intended to win complete independence for Israel.

War and Horror

World War II continued until 1945, and the war years frustrated Golda terribly. She desperately wanted the **Yishuv** to help the Jews who the Nazis were **persecuting** in Europe. But Britain was blocking Jewish **immigration** from Nazi-occupied Europe. It sent soldiers to guard the Palestinian coast and prevented Jewish refugee ships from leaving Europe. At the beginning of the war, however, neither Golda nor the British had any idea what was really happening to Jews and other **minorities** in German territory. It was not just **discrimination.** It was much worse.

Illegal immigration

The **Histadrut** believed that, to show support for European Jews, it could justify helping Jews enter Palestine illegally. Golda became closely involved with **underground** attempts to smuggle Jews into Jewish areas of Palestine, out of sight of British officials.

Not surprisingly, little trust existed between British and Jewish leaders. On one occasion, the British army accused members of the **Haganah** of stealing its weapons. Authorities called Golda Meyerson to give evidence in the case, and she amazed the court with her sarcastic replies to the British lawyer.

Key dates: world at war

1933	• January	Adolf Hitler comes to power in Germany
1939	• September	World War II begins
1939–1945		Millions of Jews die in the **Holocaust**
1945	• September	End of World War II
1948	• May 14	Israel declares its independence

▲ *During World War II, Arabs and Jews living in Palestine volunteered to fight for the British. Here, they march side by side during a training exercise in 1940.*

She defended the rights of all Jews to arm themselves against attack, from wherever their weapons might come. Her performance greatly impressed the Yishuv leaders.

Jewish fighters

Despite all this, Britain still governed the Yishuv, and large numbers of Palestinian Jews fought for the **Allies** during the war. The Histadrut was deeply opposed to Hitler and his regime. Its members hoped that Britain would reward the Jews for their efforts by granting them independence when the war ended.

In 1943, the Histadrut even persuaded Britain to let it parachute-drop 42 Jewish soldiers (mainly Haganah volunteers) behind enemy lines. The Haganah wanted to free Allied prisoners and support Jews who were opposing Hitler. Although they had some success, most of the volunteers were killed in the exercise, and Golda lost several close friends.

The Holocaust

As the war went on, rumors about what was happening in Europe began to reach Palestine. Jewish people who had escaped reported that the Nazis were rounding up Jews and taking them to prison camps, where they were tortured, killed, or used in horrible medical experiments. When the Jewish leaders first heard these stories, they decided to send investigators to try to find out more. Golda happened to

▼ *On May 7, 1945, at the end of World War II, allied armies liberated these starving prisoners at Ebensee concentration camp in Austria.*

mention this to a British official that she knew. He was amazed that she took the rumors seriously. "You must not believe everything you hear," he told her kindly.

It was all true, however. The **Allies** eventually defeated the Nazis, and as the war drew to a close in 1944 and 1945, people were discovering the full horror of what was happening to the Jews. The Nazis had herded millions of Jews into concentration camps such as Buchenwald and Dachau. The Nazis then put them to work as slaves, and starved and tortured them. In Auschwitz and other so-called death camps, the Nazis executed millions of prisoners. Altogether, the Nazis murdered more than six million Jews and members of other minorities in this terrible **genocide,** which people call the **Holocaust.**

After the war, the Jews were sure their time had come. They had suffered enough— surely the British would now allow the surviving Jewish **refugees** to come to Palestine. But the opposite was the case. The British government clamped down on the **Histadrut,** arresting many of its leaders for their disobedience during the war. Now the time came to fight for freedom.

The Nazi concentration camps

Beginning in 1933, dozens of concentration camps opened, mainly in Germany, Austria, and Poland. At first, Nazis used prisoners for labor, but in 1941 they began to build *Vernichtungslager,* or death camps, in Poland. The Nazis designed these death camps, including Auschwitz, Treblinka, and Sobibor, to execute as many Jews and other **minorities** as possible. The Nazis used gas chambers for their killing. They then burned the dead in huge ovens called crematoriums or dumped them into mass graves.

Israel Is Born!

In June 1946, Great Britain wanted to control the **Yishuv** and stop **immigration.** The British arrested many **Va'ad Hapoel** members (their leader, David Ben-Gurion, went abroad to avoid arrest). They did not arrest Golda Meyerson, however. For some reason, the British did not think she posed a threat. Or perhaps they did not want to anger the Jewish public by detaining one of the Yishuv's most popular politicians. Either way, in 1946 Golda became the acting head of Va'ad Hapoel and the unofficial leader of the Yishuv.

FOR DETAILS ON KEY PEOPLE OF MEIR'S TIME, SEE PAGE 58.

Peaceful protests

Many Jews in Palestine were prepared to fight the British with weapons. Members of the **Haganah** went into hiding and launched attacks on British officers. But Golda lived in the hope of a peaceful solution. Instead of military attacks, she

▼ *Many Jews who had escaped from the concentration camps wanted to move to Israel but ended up in a British prison on the island of Cyprus in 1946. Here, a group of Jews protest with a sign that reads: "From lager (prison camp) to lager—till when?"*

▶ *Women take an oath as they become members of the Haganah, the Jewish secret army, in Tel Aviv in 1948.*

organized street protests and civil disobedience against the British. The latter involved peacefully refusing to obey British laws—a tactic that people in India were also using against British control.

On one occasion, Golda even took part in a hunger strike. The British were refusing to allow two ships filled with Jewish **refugees** to sail to Palestine from Italy. The refugees went on a hunger strike, and Golda persuaded the Yishuv leaders to join them. They went without food for days, until the British allowed the ships to leave.

Crackdown

Still, the British did not give in to the Jewish demand for a **homeland.** Instead, in 1947 they started to arrest illegal Jewish immigrants. They then took them to offshore prison camps, such as the one on the island of Cyprus. These actions infuriated the Jews, and the violence and civil disobedience grew. The situation was becoming impossible.

Finally, the **United Nations** (UN), an international organization formed just after the war, took control. It set up a committee to debate the situation in Palestine and to vote on its future. On November 29, 1947, the committee voted in favor of the separation of Palestine into a Jewish state and an Arab state. The Jews accepted this but the **Arabs** did not.

War worries

The UN vote delighted the **Yishuv** leaders, who the British had now freed from prison. But the Yishuv leaders knew that if the UN granted them independence, this would anger the **Arab** countries in the area. The new Jewish state would probably have to fight its neighbors to establish its borders, and to do so it needed support from abroad.

David Ben-Gurion, leader of **Mapai,** Israel's leading political party, was planning to visit the United States to ask for help. But Golda pointed out that the Jews at home needed his leadership. So, in January 1948, the **Va'ad Hapoel** members voted that Golda should go instead. She had proved herself to be a brilliant fundraiser, she had friends in the United States, and she spoke fluent English. She set off immediately.

David Ben-Gurion

Born in Plonsk, Poland, in 1886, David Ben-Gurion was a lifelong **Zionist.** He arrived in Palestine in 1906 and became involved in the early **kibbutz** movement and with the **Histadrut.** As leader of the Histadrut and the Mapai Party, he became Israel's first prime minister in 1948 and held the post twice before retiring in 1963. Nicknamed "the Old Man" in later life, he died in 1973, at the age of 87.

Golda's missions

In the United States, Golda Meyerson raised an astonishing $50 million for the new Jewish state. Americans—especially American Jews—responded generously by the thousands to her powerful and emotional speeches. This money made it possible to set up the new country. On her return, Golda undertook more missions—

some of which were secret and highly dangerous. She went to visit King Abdullah of Jordan, one of the Arab countries closest to the Yishuv, in an attempt to **negotiate** peace with the Arabs.

A declaration of independence

In the spring of 1948, David Ben-Gurion was ready to declare independence. It was a risk. The British would not support the Jews, and they would probably have to fight several Arab nations. But with support, money, and arms from the United States, they thought they had a chance. So, on May 14, 1948, Ben-Gurion officially proclaimed the new state of Israel at a ceremony in Tel Aviv. Ben-Gurion became the country's first prime minister.

▲ David Ben-Gurion, prime minister of the new state of Israel (center right, wearing jacket), watches the final withdrawal of the British government from Israel in Haifa in July 1948.

Golda remembered the ceremony as an emotional occasion. "The State of Israel!" she later wrote in her autobiography. "My eyes filled with tears, and my hands shook. We had done it! We had brought the Jewish state into existence—and I, Golda Mabovitch Meyerson, had lived to see the day."

The United States recognized the new state almost immediately. But trouble lay ahead. The very next day, Israel came under attack from six of its Arab neighbors: Jordan, Egypt, Saudi Arabia, Syria, Lebanon, and Iraq. The war of independence had begun.

In Government

The new state of Israel, just a few days old, was under siege. Jerusalem became a battleground. Arab **snipers** lined the road between Jerusalem and Tel Aviv, and war raged along Israel's new borders. But Golda was sure that Israel would win the war. She wanted to be where the action was and hoped for a place in the new Israeli **cabinet.** During a visit to the United States in June 1948, however, she found out that Israeli leaders had appointed her as the **ambassador** to Moscow.

The assignment disappointed Golda. The job would isolate her from her colleagues and prevent her from helping with the war effort. Nevertheless, she responded to the call of duty—despite having broken her leg in a taxi crash before leaving the United States. By September 1948, she was in Moscow.

Winning the war

Although Golda could not be there, the money and support she had raised helped Israel's war effort. Israel won the war of independence in January 1949. Talks took place to draw up peace treaties. An Israeli election also took place, and voters returned Ben-Gurion to power. He served from 1948 to 1953, when he temporarily retired from office. He appointed Golda minister of labor in his cabinet. The new government then recalled her from Moscow.

◄ Prime Minister David Ben-Gurion and foreign minister Golda Meir at a meeting with the leader of the **United Nations,** Dag Hammarskjöld (far right), in 1957.

The duties of minister of labor were similar to those that Golda had undertaken for the **Histadrut** twenty years earlier. They included organizing jobs, homes, and training for thousands of Jewish immigrants, whom Israel was now able to welcome with open arms. Golda also went on many more fundraising trips to Europe and the United States.

Foreign minister

Golda performed so well, especially on her trips abroad, that Israel's leaders began to realize she was worthy of an even more important job. In 1956, they appointed her foreign minister—a position second in command only to Ben-Gurion, who had returned to power and would serve until 1963. However, another reason existed for the appointment. Ben-Gurion wanted to rid himself of Moshe Sharrett, the previous prime minister from 1953 to 1955. Ben-Gurion wanted to attack the **Arab** states, but the more liberal Sharrett favored coming to a peaceful agreement with them. Golda preferred talking over fighting, too, but Ben-Gurion thought she would be less trouble than Sharrett. Golda not only had to perform the duties of her new job, but she also had to deal with her old friend Sharrett's anger at being pushed aside.

FOR DETAILS ON KEY PEOPLE OF MEIR'S TIME, SEE PAGE 58.

The war of independence

Israel's war of independence began on May 15, 1948, when six Arab countries—Egypt, Syria, Jordan, Iraq, Saudi Arabia, and Lebanon—attacked their new neighbor. The Arab armies had more fighters and more equipment, but communication among the countries was poor. Although the Arab fighters outnumbered Israel's army, it was well organized and well trained. The fighting took place in small bursts, with cease-fires in between, until Israel had taken over more land than it had started with. In January 1949, the war officially ended, but many Arab states remained hostile toward Israel.

At this time, Golda changed her last name. Israeli policy dictated that senior members of the government were expected to have **Hebrew** names to reflect the country's policy of using Hebrew as its official language. Golda picked the name *Meir,* meaning "illuminate," partly because it resembled her old name.

Big responsibilities

Throughout her life, Golda Meir proved she could do any job that was handed to her. Dealing with disagreements inside the government and with other countries made the role of foreign minister hard work. But Meir succeeded, drawing on all her courage, **charisma,** and **diplomatic** skill. She traveled the world, representing the new country on visits to dozens of countries, conferences, and committees.

An important canal

The Suez Crisis occurred because the British and French angered Nasser for withdrawing their money, which he needed to build Egypt's Aswan Dam. Nasser wanted Egypt to become independent and thought he could achieve this by aligning himself with the Soviet Union rather than the United States. By seizing control of the Suez Canal, he denied the Europeans an important trade route to India and the rest of Asia. Israel also needed the Suez Canal, and the nearby Straits of Tiran, to reach Israel's southernmost tip by sea.

In July 1956, during Meir's term as foreign minister, the Suez Crisis occurred. The dispute centered over control of the Suez Canal, which links the Mediterranean and Red seas. The Suez Canal Company, nearly half-owned by Britain, controlled the canal. Egypt's president, Gamal Abdel-Nasser, **nationalized** the canal, and Britain and France secretly joined forces with Israel to try to take it back. The Israeli army was successful and took over a large area of Egyptian territory, but the **United Nations** ordered that it be given back. The two sides reached a compromise, but Meir felt let down by the UN and by her old friend, the United States. She spent much of the rest of her time as foreign minister rebuilding Israel's relationship with the United States. She also visited Africa and developed relationships with many of the countries there.

Personal problems

Although her career had reached its highest point so far, this was a difficult time in Meir's private life. In 1951, her estranged husband Morris had died. He was staying at her home in Jerusalem at the time, but typically she was away on business. Her mother died the same year, her daughter Sarah became sick again, and Golda herself was not in good health. By 1965, she was exhausted and wanted to spend more time being a mother and grandmother. She decided to retire as foreign minister, but she remained in the position of secretary-general of her party. Little did she know that even greater career success awaited her.

FOR DETAILS ON KEY PEOPLE OF MEIR'S TIME, SEE PAGE 58.

▼ *The people of Port Said in Egypt wander the streets after an attack by British and French troops during the Suez Crisis.*

Israel's Problems

Israel won the first war against its **Arab** neighbors in 1949, but its problems were far from over. Arab groups in and around Palestine still launched attacks against Israeli citizens, and Israel's leaders argued fiercely with one another about what to do in response. Meanwhile, the Arab nations still planned to take back land now in Israel, which they saw as theirs by right. When Meir retired as foreign minister in 1965, the state of no war and no peace continued. Several Arab states prepared themselves for another battle against Israel.

▼ *In a rare moment of relaxation, foreign minister Golda Meir plays with her grandchildren in Israel in 1961.*

A new prime minister

Prime Minister Ben-Gurion retired in 1963, and **Mapai** Party. members chose Levi Eshkol to replace him as head of the party. Meir was secretary-general of Mapai. But soon after Eshkol took over the leadership, Ben-Gurion and Eshkol had a disagreement.

FOR DETAILS ON KEY PEOPLE OF MEIR'S TIME, SEE PAGE 58.

Power behind the throne

Although she had retired as foreign minister, Meir still played an important role in Israeli politics. As secretary-general of the Mapai Party, she found that government leaders came to her for advice on international issues. They also reported on progress to her—not the prime minister. Even Eshkol asked her advice.

More war on the way

In May 1967, Egypt again closed off the Straits of Tiran, the southern sea route vital to Israel. Israel viewed this act as a declaration of war. It would have to battle Egypt to win control of the straits, and other Arab states were poised to join Egypt in this fight. Egypt, Syria, and Jordan were all placing weapons and fighter planes on Israel's borders.

The Israeli people wanted Eshkol to attack Egypt immediately. When he failed to do so, they called for the appointment of the former head of the Israeli Defense Forces, Moshe Dayan, as defense minister. Meir did not want this. She wanted a peaceful solution and would have preferred to **negotiate** with the Arabs. On the other hand, she was confident that Israel had the power to win the coming war. Eventually, the government bowed to public pressure and, at the beginning of June 1967, Dayan became defense minister. On June 5, he launched lightning strikes on Arab air bases to destroy their waiting aircraft before they could takeoff. Israel was at war again.

▲ *An Egyptian fighter plane, destroyed by Israeli forces during the Six-Day War in 1967, lies wrecked on the ground at El Arish, Egypt.*

The Six-Day War

This war lasted just six days, from June 5 to June 10, and became one of the most famous in Israel's short history. The unexpected Israeli strikes weakened the **Arabs** and left them unable to launch the attacks they had planned. Israel's aggressive action not only protected their interests, but also enabled them to take over new lands more than three times the size of their existing territory. Israel now controlled more than a million Arabs living in these areas. The Jews now controlled parts of Jerusalem that the Arabs had previously controlled. Parts of Jerusalem that became open to the Jews again included the Western Wall, an ancient Jewish holy site.

The whole country united in rejoicing, and Israelis hailed Dayan as a hero. Meanwhile, Meir focused on a new task. The war had divided the **Mapai** Party, and it had split into two separate groups. Through many meetings, Meir managed to create a new party—the **Labor** Party.

Meir now decided that it really was time to take a backseat. She stepped down as secretary-general in July 1968 and prepared to spend more time with her family and friends.

Too much for Eshkol

Throughout this time, Prime Minister Eshkol had been sick, and he died on February 26, 1969. Following the success of the Six-Day War, Moshe Dayan was popular with the public and could have stepped into Eshkol's shoes. But many in the Labor Party did not want such a hard-line politician and a member of the younger generation at the top. They wanted a wise, moderate leader who could hold the party together until events had calmed down. Soon after Eshkol's death, many members of the party begged Meir to take over—just until the government could hold public elections in October.

Although Meir had tried on numerous occasions to retire, the lure of politics always called her back. Doctors had diagnosed her with cancer, yet the needs of her country meant everything to her. She consulted with her children and her nephew Yonah, Shenya's son, who all said she should take the job. Finally, she was ready to accept the leadership. The Labor Party members held a vote, and they elected Meir the party leader. Not one person cast a vote against her. She became prime minister of Israel on March 7, 1969.

On becoming prime minister

When people elected her prime minister, Meir later said, she was in shock. "I know that tears rolled down my cheeks and that I held my head in my hands when the voting was over," she recalled. "I was dazed. I had never planned to be prime minister."

Prime Minister Meir

Leading Israel in 1969 was not an easy task. Acts of **terrorism** were still commonplace. In the week that Meir took office, a bomb exploded in a student café in Jerusalem, injuring 29 people. Meir often found herself attending funerals for victims of terrorism. And, although this was a time of relative peace, Israel's armies were constantly defending the borders of the new territories that they had taken over in the Six-Day War.

American support

One of Meir's first actions as prime minister was her famous state visit to the United States. U.S. president Richard M. Nixon had been reluctant to help Israel with more weapons and money. However, when he met with Meir, she managed to persuade him to sell modern fighting equipment to her country. She also made public speeches and held **press conferences,** and her popularity with the American public seemed to be greater than ever.

Israel had the military power to succeed in war largely because of Meir's good relationship with the United States, and for this the Israeli public rated her highly. By the time the government held elections in October 1969, Israelis no longer saw Meir as a stand-in. They elected her with a huge majority.

▶ *Election posters featuring Golda Meir are displayed in Jerusalem during the Israeli elections in October 1969.*

Life at the top

At 71 years of age, Meir now found herself with a busier schedule than ever before. The long hours and her poor health left her exhausted, and she often slept during the day after working late into the night. Her eyesight was failing,

▲ *The new prime minister gives a speech at a Labor Party Conference in Tel Aviv in 1970.*

so she relied heavily on her two close aides, Lou Kaddar and Simcha Dinitz, to read important **telegrams** to her. They also had to schedule all her public appointments while still allowing her time to spend with her family. Once, when she wanted to meet her younger sister Clara at the airport but was tied up with work, the stress became too much for her. She hurled an ashtray across the room. She later apologized, but her aides learned not to make the same mistake again.

The Kitchen Cabinet

As always, Meir mixed work with home life. On every Monday a formal **cabinet** meeting took place, so on Sunday nights she would invite her party colleagues to her house to discuss policy. These informal meetings became known as Golda's Kitchen Cabinet. She even took the role of a traditional Jewish grandmother, making chicken soup for her younger male colleagues. Yet, no one underestimated her. She was always in control.

Peace and prosperity

With Meir's influence, financial and military support came from the United States. The Israeli government was able to focus on nonmilitary issues, such as improving housing and employment opportunities for Israelis and developing the tourist industry.

Meir also hoped to begin peace talks with the **Arab** states—especially Egypt and Jordan. She had always believed that it would be better to **negotiate** with the Arabs rather than fight wars with them. She held secret talks with King Hussein of Jordan. But Hussein wanted Israel to return all the land it had taken in 1967, and the two leaders could not agree. Meanwhile, the **Palestine Liberation Organization (PLO)** was gaining in strength under a new leader, Yasser Arafat.

Nonetheless, Israel felt good about itself. It had international support, and its borders were strong. As Yitzhak Rabin, who would one day be prime minister himself, put it: "Golda Meir has better boundaries than King David or King Solomon." So, when war broke out again in 1973, it came as a surprise.

The Yom Kippur War

This war broke out on Yom Kippur, one of the holiest days in the Jewish calendar. In 1973, Yom Kippur fell on Saturday, October 6. A slight air of tension existed in Israel—military leaders had warned that armies were gathering in Syria. But most people agreed that Syria was not planning to attack.

However, at 4:00 A.M. on the day before Yom Kippur, the Israeli military received a warning that Egypt and Syria would declare war the next day at 6:00 P.M. When Meir heard the news, she knew she had to mobilize forces in both northern

▲ *Golda Meir inspects an honor guard in Tel Aviv in October 1970, just before leaving for a meeting of the* **United Nations** *in New York.*

and southern Israel. Despite the warning, she did not want Israel to attack first because this would make the Israelis appear aggressive, and that might make the United States withdraw its support. Eventually, the Arab countries launched attacks at around 1:00 P.M. on October 6, and Israel suffered heavy losses. Meir managed to get help from the United States once again, and Israel finally beat back the attack. The two sides declared a cease-fire on October 25.

Time to go

When Israel held elections in late 1973, voters reelected the **Labor** Party. Meir won support from her colleagues to continue as prime minister. However, many people wanted to know why she had not seen the Yom Kippur War coming, and why more than 2,500 Israeli soldiers had lost their lives. Although an official inquiry said that she had acted properly throughout, the Yom Kippur War racked her with guilt. She was also old, tired, and still battling cancer. The time had come to retire.

After forming a new **cabinet,** Meir formally resigned from her post as prime minister and from her seat in the **Knesset** (the Israeli parliament) on April 10, 1974.

▲ *Prime Minister Meir meets with newly arrived Jewish immigrants from the Soviet Union in Jerusalem in June 1971.*

Meir in power

1963	• June	David Ben-Gurion resigns as prime minister, appointing Levi Eshkol in his place
1969	• February	Meir replaces Eshkol as prime minister
1969	• September	Meir visits the United States to raise support for Israel
1973	• October	Many Israelis die in the Yom Kippur War
1974	• April	Meir resigns as prime minister

Golda Meir's Legacy

In 1978, just four years after stepping down as prime minister, the 80-year-old Meir died in Jerusalem of the cancer she had fought for fifteen years. She had spent her retirement writing her autobiography, *My Life,* traveling widely, and staying active in politics as an adviser to her former colleagues. At the time of her death, people all over the world admired her as a wise, tough, and unique politician. But what did she leave behind?

Peace in Israel?

All her life, Meir had longed for a Jewish **homeland** where her people could live in peace. She wanted Jews to live in harmony with their **Arab** neighbors and with all other peoples and cultures. But when it came to defending Israel, she was prepared to fight. She believed that Israel had a right to exist and that if other countries or people attacked Israel, it had a right to defend itself.

▼ *Still busy after her retirement, Meir laughs during a meeting with U.S. president Gerald Ford at the White House in 1975.*

▲ *Friends and supporters follow Golda Meir's coffin at her state funeral in Jerusalem in December 1978.*

In the end, Jews and **Arabs** did not achieve peace in the Middle East during Meir's lifetime. In that sense, she did not achieve her aims. Like other people of her generation, she did not recognize the importance of the Palestinians. She once said: "There is no such thing as a Palestinian." However, she did play a major role in creating the state of Israel. Her hard work at the **Histadrut,** her devotion to the struggle against the British, and most of all, her amazing ability to raise funds and support from abroad were all vital to the survival of the Jewish state in its first few years.

A woman's work

Perhaps equally importantly, Meir played a huge part in breaking down the barriers that prevented women from achieving political power. She showed that if someone was the best person for a job, whether that person was male or female did not matter.

When people asked her if she was a **feminist,** however, she often said she did not agree with all aspects of feminism. She had always taken her role as a wife and mother seriously and had always worried about neglecting it for her career. Although many feminists regarded her as a hero, she never promoted feminism for its own sake. She said simply that men and women had to work together. Since her time at Kibbutz Merhavia, where everyone shared equally in the work, she never saw why being a woman should make any difference. She wanted people to remember her as a great politician— not a great female politician.

Goodbye, Golda

Meir's obituary in the *New York Times* on December 9, 1978, concluded: "At the end of her life she was still feeling guilty about the years during which she had neglected her children and about her failure to devote herself to the **kibbutz** rather than to public life." She once wrote: "There is a type of woman who cannot remain at home. In spite of the place her children and family fill in her life, her nature demands something more; she cannot divorce herself from the larger social life. She cannot let her children narrow her horizon. For such a woman, there is no rest."

Timeline

1898	Born in Kiev, Russia
1903	Golda's father Moshe Mabovitch goes to the United States to find work
1905	Family joins Moshe in Milwaukee, Wisconsin
1913	Runs away to Denver, Colorado, to live with Shenya
1917	Marries Morris Meyerson Balfour Declaration states that Britain is in favor of a Jewish **homeland** in Palestine
1921	Golda and Morris move to Palestine and join **Kibbutz** Merhavia
1924	Golda and Morris move to Jerusalem to work for the **Histadrut** (national labor union) and son Menachem is born
1926	Daughter Sarah is born
1928	Takes a job with Women's Labor Council of the Histadrut
1930s	Jewish **immigration** to Palestine increases as European Jews flee German territories
1932	Works as a campaigner and fundraiser for the **Yishuv** (Jewish settlement of Palestine)
1933	Adolf Hitler comes to power in Germany
1939	British restrict Jewish immigration to Palestine World War II breaks out
1944	The full extent of the **Holocaust** (mass murder of European Jews) is revealed

1945	End of World War II
1946	Acts as temporary leader of the Histadrut
1947	The **United Nations** votes in favor of an independent Jewish state in Palestine
1948	Raises $50 million in the United States for the Israeli independence effort Israel declares independence Becomes Israel's ambassador to Moscow
1949	Israel wins the war of independence against its Arab neighbors Becomes minister of labor
1956	Becomes Israeli foreign minister Changes her name to Golda Meir Suez Crisis erupts
1963	David Ben-Gurion resigns as prime minister and appoints Levi Eshkol in his place
1965	Resigns as foreign minister
1967	Israel wins the Six-Day War
1969	Resigns as secretary-general of the **Labor Party** Appointed temporary prime minister Undertakes a U.S. state visit and tour Israelis elect Golda Meir prime minister
1973	Israel suffers heavy losses in the Yom Kippur War The Labor Party is reelected with Meir as prime minister
1974	Resigns as prime minister
1978	Dies in Jerusalem

Key People of Meir's Time

Ben-Gurion, David (1886–1973) Ben-Gurion was a leading **Zionist** and Israel's first prime minister. Born in Poland, he moved to Palestine in 1909. He was a founding member of the **kibbutz** movement and of the **Histadrut.** As head of the **Mapai** Party, he led the struggle to establish Israel as an independent state and became prime minister after Israel declared independence in May 1948. After a short break in the mid-1950s, he returned to power and finally resigned as Israeli leader in 1963.

Eshkol, Levi (1895–1969) Eshkol was Israel's prime minister from 1963 to 1969. Eshkol was born in Kiev, Russia, and moved to Palestine in 1914. He worked as a Zionist campaigner and farmer and joined the **Haganah** (**underground** army) in 1940. After Israel became independent, he served as agriculture minister and finance minister before being installed as prime minister in 1963. He died while still in office.

Herzl, Theodor (1860–1904) A founder of modern **Zionism** (the belief in a Jewish homeland), Herzl was born in Hungary and worked as a journalist in Paris. He spread Zionism through his conferences and publications and founded the World Zionist Organization in 1897. In 1904 he died at the young age of 44, long before the state of Israel came into being.

Hitler, Adolf (1889–1945) Founder and leader of the **Nazi Party,** which came to power in Germany in 1933, he ordered the **persecution** and murder of six million Jews and the killing of many other **minority** groups. His invasion of lands around Germany led to the outbreak of World War II in 1939.

King Hussein (1935–1999) Hussein was the king of Jordan, Israel's neighbor, and, after 1994, its closest friend in the Arab world. Hussein's grandfather King Abdullah was assassinated in 1951. After his father King Talal resigned because of poor health, Hussein became king in 1952 at the age of sixteen. He was well known for his attempts to **negotiate** peace in the Middle East.

Abdel-Nasser, Gamal (1918–1970) Egypt's president from 1954 to 1970, Nasser rose from a poor background to lead his country. His **nationalization** of the Suez Canal in 1956 led to the Suez Crisis, involving Israel, Great Britain, and France, and he was instrumental in starting the Six-Day War against Israel in 1967. He died of a heart attack while still in office.

Nixon, Richard M. (1913–1994) Nixon was the U.S. president from 1969 to 1974, at the same time as Golda Meir was Israel's leader. Nixon gave Israel much-needed financial and military support after Meir's state visit to the United States in 1969. He was forced to resign from office after a scandal in 1974.

Sadat, Anwar (1918–1981) Egyptian leader from 1970 to 1981, Sadat led Egypt into the Yom Kippur War with Israel in 1973. He later negotiated a peace deal with Israeli leader Menachem Begin, for which they shared the Nobel Prize for peace in 1978. **Muslim** extremists, who were against the deal, assassinated him in 1981.

Sources for Further Research

Altman, Linda Jacobs. *The Creation of Israel*. Farmington Hills, Mich.: Gale Group, 1998.

Hitzeroth, Deborah. *Golda Meir* ("The Importance of" series). London: Greenhaven Press, 1997.

Marsh, Carole. *Golda Meir: A Wisconsin Experience Reader*. Peachtree City, Ga.: Gallopade International, 2001.

McAuley, Karen. *Golda Meir*. Collingdale, Pa.: Diane Publishing, 1997.

McCullough, L. E. *Israel Reborn: Legends of the Diaspora and Israel's Modern Rebirth*. Lyme, N.H.: Smith & Kraus, Incorporated, 2000.

Resling, Darlene E. *Golda Meir: A Play*. Baltimore: Learning Well, 1997.

Schachter, Sarah and Fishman, Priscilla. *A Young Person's History of Israel*. Springfield, N.J.: Behrman House, 1995.

Silverman, Maida. *Israel: The Founding of a Modern Nation*. New York: Penguin Putnam, 2001.

Glossary

Allies group of countries—Great Britain, the United States, France, Australia, New Zealand, the Soviet Union, and others—that fought together in World War II against the Axis powers (Germany, Italy, and Japan)

ambassador politician sent abroad to represent the country

Arabs group of peoples from countries in the Middle East and North Africa

cabinet group made up of senior members of a government

charisma personal style that attracts and influences other people

communal shared between a group of people

cossack soldier who served the czar during the Russian Empire

czar title of the monarch, or ruler, in the Russian Empire

diaspora widespread distribution of peoples around the world, especially the movements of Jews following the conquest of Jerusalem and the destruction of the Jewish temple by the Romans more than 2,000 years ago

diplomatic concerning relations between the governments of different countries

discrimination unfavorable treatment based on prejudice, especially because of race, religion, or gender

executive committee small group of people that controls a political party, company, or other organization

exodus historic departure of the Israelites from Egypt

feminist follower of a movement that developed during the 1900s that aims to bring about financial and social equality for women and men

genocide killing of large numbers of people on the basis of their nationality or race

ghetto area of a town or city where a particular group of people—often an ethnic minority—live together

gypsies European name for the Roma, an ethnic group that originally came from northern India and now lives in many parts of Europe

Haganah secret underground Jewish army founded in 1920 to defend Jews against Arab attacks

Hebrew original ancient language of the Jews, revived in the 1900s as the official language of Israel

Histadrut Jewish national labor union founded in 1920 to help Jewish settlers in Palestine find work

Holocaust mass torture and extermination of Jews and other minorities carried out by the Nazi regime in Europe in the 1930s and 1940s

homeland area of land that an ethnic group or nation sees as its rightful home

immigration moving to one country from another to live there permanently

kibbutz Israeli farm on which members share everything equally

Knesset Israeli parliament

Labor Israeli political party (previously known as the Mapai Party) of which Golda Meir was the leader when she came to power in 1969

Mapai Israeli socialist political party that was founded in 1930 and led the process of making Israel an independent country. After splitting, it became the Labor Party in 1968.

messiah in Jewish tradition, a person who will deliver the Jews from suffering and reign over a new kingdom of Israel

minority small group within a larger group or nation

Muslim follower of Islam and Muhammad the prophet

mutiny rebellion by the crew against the captain of a ship

nationalization process of taking over industries and resources so that they are owned and run by a country as a whole, instead of by private companies

Nazi Party National Socialist Party, led by Adolf Hitler, which came to power in Germany in 1933 and promoted prejudice against and persecution of Jews and other minorities

negotiate to talk with another person or group in order to reach an agreement

Ottoman Empire large area covering parts of Europe, Africa, and Asia, controlled by the Turks for several hundred years before being taken apart after World War I

Palestine Liberation Organization (PLO) group set up by several Arab countries in 1964 to oppose the state of Israel and help Palestinian Arabs fight to set up their own country

peninsula strip of land with water on three sides

persecution violent treatment or harassment of a person or group, especially on the basis of their race or religion

pogrom type of organized riot, common in Russia in the late 1800s, in which mobs rampaged through Jewish areas, killing Jews and destroying their property

press conference meeting in which politicians or other newsworthy people talk to journalists and answer their questions

promised land the part of the Middle East from which the Jews originally came and which, according to Jewish beliefs, God had promised to them

refugee a person who flees a country to escape danger or persecution

right wing in politics, tending toward conservative values such as the importance of tradition and the power of the individual, rather than the state

skirmishes short battles

sniper person who fires shots from a hidden position

socialism political system originally based on equality and the fair distribution of a country's wealth among its people

socialist someone who believes in the equal distribution of wealth among the members of a society

steerage cheapest quarters on a passenger liner, usually located on the lower decks at the back of the ship

telegram early type of long distance communication, transmitted by sending electrical signals along cables

terrorism using or threatening violent attacks in an attempt to win political change

tuberculosis infectious disease, usually of the lungs

underground army or political group that operates in secret

United Nations (UN) international organization set up at the end of World War II, in 1945, to encourage peace and communication between the nations of the world

Va'ad Hapoel ruling committee of the Histadrut

white paper official government report or proposal on a particular issue

Yiddish traditional Jewish language spoken by many Jews in different parts of the world

Yishuv Jewish settlement in Palestine before independence

Zionism belief in the creation of a Jewish homeland

Zionist follower of Zionism

Index